EVENT PLANNING

PLAN EVENTS LIKE A PROFESSIONAL. IMPRESS YOUR CLIENTS AND BE YOUR OWN BOSS IN 12 SIMPLE STEPS

Disclaimer

This book is only intended as an informational guideline to become an event planner, and should not be considered expert instruction. All attempts have been made to verify the information listed in this book; however, the author cannot assume any responsibility for any loss, damage or misappropriation of any information herein contained.

Introduction

Event planning is something that most people will eventually be confronted with in their lives – in personal and professional capacities. Sometimes it falls on your plate unexpectedly, when you're requested by your boss to arrange an "intimate evening" for 100 potential clients, causing you to have a minor panic attack; or you're put in charge as a best man or maid of honour, and all of a sudden need to throw a bachelor party for 50 people; or you just want your child to have an incredible 10th birthday party. Some of you may even be considering event planning as a profession, and need some building blocks to start on.

This book covers all of those bases as a beginner's guide to event planning. By the time you're done reading it, you'll have a great holistic idea of how to approach your event. Otherwise, because the book is broken up into easy-to-follow steps covering each of the main components of event planning, you can also use it as a referral in areas you are uncertain about, or as a refresher when you are trying something new you are unfamiliar with.

Included with the steps is a comprehensive checklist for both small and big events, as well as a comprehensive checklist for weddings, which you can use every time you plan an event to ensure you have everything covered. You can even add to these checklists to customise them to suit your specific needs and area of planning!

So are you ready to plan an unforgettable event? Let's get started!

Contents

Chapter 1
What you need to know

This chapter is all about looking at what an event planner actually does, and what you will be exploring in further detail later on in this guide.

The ultimate event planner:

Do you have the flair and enthusiasm for putting together not just an event, but an experience? Do you love to not only see the bigger picture but also find excitement in the well-thought-out smaller details that make any event a whopping success? Are you a creative soul that delights in making other's dreams a reality? And probably the most important question…are you so great at organising that even your vegetable rack is organised alphabetically (ok, so not quite there)? Then you have all the key qualities to becoming the ultimate event planner!

A few key notes you will need to keep in mind

- You are going to plan, design and produce awesome events while managing all the nitty-gritty project elements within (sometimes crazy) time limits.
- Stroke up a conversation and have a serious heart to heart with your over-eager clients! Identify their souls desires and get creative while still being professional.
- Check out what other events are making waves and gaining success! Marketing research is a game changer!
- You will need to put your game face on and negotiate contracts prior to closing any slick deals.

- Let those involved know what's going on as often as possible, show them you're in control and on top of it.
- Propose your own ideas to make the big event day a massive success, get crazy and get creative!
- Remember that nitty-gritty I mentioned? You will need to organise facilities and manage all event's details such as decor, catering, entertainment, transportation, location, invitee list, special guests, equipment, promotional material etc...phew! But you can do it!
- Keep in mind the serious stuff, like insurance, legal, health and safety obligations
- Show them how its done! Specify staff requirements and coordinate their activities
- Contact someone that's great with marketing and a bit of PR if need be, creating hype could make or break your event, depending on what you've planned for.
- Plan for problems, if something is going to go wrong, like the white doves you had planned for a mid-speech flight decided to take a sick day...be quick on your feet and grab that confetti! As long as you act with confidence and use your best judgement you're good to go.
- You will need to be able to time manage like a boss, but with this helpful guide, we've got you covered.
- And if you're going into your own business, a few snazzy sale skills wouldn't hurt.

The cornerstone of great event planning is organisation. Unfortunately, life has its own way of going, and the unexpected happens quite often. This is why it's so important to plan well!

It might seem overwhelming to deal with a big event, because there are so many components to it – but never try to handle it as a whole. That's why we break it down onto manageable chunks, listed in Chapter 2 as 12 simple steps. If each small step is executed, nothing will be able to shake you on the big day.

If you're ready to upskill, change your career or just completely wow your friends at your next get-together, then let's get going with chapter 2 and the 12 simple steps!

Chapter 2
A step-by-step guide to plan events like a pro

Each of these steps isolates a component of event planning. The type of event you are planning will determine how many of these steps you need to follow. For instance, if you are planning a wedding, you will not need to build the event up with publicity. While this is a holistic guide, catering for all types of events, you can tailor it to suit your needs if you are only looking at sticking to one type of event, like kids' parties or fundraisers – which may be the wise choice if event planning is your chosen career path. Like many veteran planners will tell you, dealing with brides on a regular basis requires an incredible penchant for thinking on your feet, as well as the ability to deal with crisis.

Step 1: Get your act together – what are the requirements of the event?

Objectives

The first step in pulling together a successful event is determining exactly what your objectives are.

Depending on the type of event, for example a corporate get-together or a wedding, these will be very different. So take some time to think about what it is that you would like to achieve at the end of it.

Budget

Obviously, you will need to determine what kind of budget you have to work with to know on what scale you can pull off the event.

Sponsorship

If your budget is very limited, consider a sponsor or partnership for the event in the case of publicity events or fundraisers. To find a sponsor, you'll need to make a list of potential sponsors and put together a sponsorship package to send to them. Actively follow up to see if any of the potential sponsors show interest. They will have to get something out of the partnership as well, so keep this in mind when writing the proposal. Remember that you must thank your sponsor during the event, and will probably need to give them press with the event as well.

Questionnaire

Here's a quick questionnaire to help get you on your way:

Quick questionnaire	
What is the pervading feeling that the guests will leave with?	
What kind of atmosphere do you want the event to have:	

professional, romantic?	
What is the purpose of the event: press, informative?	
What are the most important things that need to happen during the event?	
What end result will mean that the event was a success?	
How much do you have to spend on the event – will it be big and glamorous or budget-friendly?	
If your budget is limited, can you organise some kind of sponsorship? If so, from whom?	

Step 2: Set a date

Before you pick a date, there are a few things you need to take into consideration:

- **Adequate time** Give yourself enough time to get everything done. Any event takes at least a few months to plan.
- **What's going on at the same time** Check if your chosen date coincides with anything else of importance, like public or school holidays, big events, much-anticipated sport matches, and so forth. You can check with the nearest visitor information centre to see what other events are scheduled. You don't want your guests to decline invitations because they have other things they have to do.
- **Make sure important people are available** If you're planning on having a speaker or VIP at your event, check that they are free on your chosen date.
- **Seasons** If you have a longer timeframe within which to have the event, think about the season. Obviously, an evening function in the middle of winter won't hold all that much appeal. If it's necessary to have an outdoor function, try not to aim for the rainiest time of year.

Step 3: Pick a venue

In case this isn't self-evident, let me take the time to stress how important the venue is. The venue is going to set the tone for the event – it is going to create the backdrop, and be the first impression people get when they arrive. The venue needs to accommodate your event very well; it absolutely has to check all the boxes.

So what are the criteria of a great venue?

- **Location** The venue needs to be easily accessible, and located within a central area, so it's close enough for most of the guests. This will usually be in the main city or town your target audience is. You don't want a place somewhere obscure or in a dangerous area, where guests won't be likely to want to go. Ensure the venue is wheelchair-friendly.
- **Transport** Make sure there are local transportation routes servicing the area in which the venue is situated, and that it is easily accessible through these routes, and check that there will be enough parking for people who drive themselves, as well as security for the parked cars (you can hire a car guard or valet service if the venue doesn't supply this). Ensure close parking spots for VIP guests and disabled persons.
- **Ambience** The atmosphere and look of the venue have to be in line with that of the event. If it's more of a quirky and fun event or party, go for an interesting venue that's guaranteed to be a talking point and be memorable. If it's more of a professional corporate event, go for a venue that has a formal, professional look.
- **History** Read reviews about the venue to make sure it has a history of good service and satisfied clients.
- **Facilities** Have a look at the facilities of the venue, and make sure they are all acceptable. Be aware of the quality of the food and service by trying them out yourself.
- **Audience** If you're throwing a kids' party, make sure all the required kids' amenities are there for them to enjoy themselves. On the other hand, if it's for a more mature audience, make sure it's easily accessible with nearby bathroom facilities.

Starting out as an event planner, you won't yet know a lot of places and which kind of events they will be suitable for, so this will be where you start building your database. If you use some of the same venues repeatedly, you can start building rapport with the owner or manager, and possibly get better future deals that way.

Step 4: Plan like there *is* a tomorrow!

TIP: Get everything confirmed in writing from the venue and vendors!

Since there are so many things to keep track of when planning an event, it is absolutely essential that you stay well organised. This means even thinking ahead enough to have back-up plans in place should there be a crisis.

To keep well organised, you'll want to keep everything you have relating to the event in one place. Draw up a calendar with your timeframe, and write down important tasks and when you need to do them. Keep a checklist to make sure you aren't forgetting anything (one is provided below). Modify the checklist to include everything you need for your event – this will be your master plan. Follow it very carefully.

If there are many components to the event, draw up a floor plan and carefully decide where everything should be set up. The layout of the event is important, so spend some time thinking about where everything should be to ensure maximum enjoyment for the guests.

Event planning checklist

Name of event:	
Date and time:	
Venue:	
Main objective:	
Number of guests:	

4-6 months before	
Set out an event plan	
Determine the budget (monitor and adjust throughout planning)	
Pick a date	
If necessary, gain approval from local government	
Pick a suitable venue and book it	
Draw up a floor plan	

Create a press/publicity plan	
Book the entertainment/speakers/activities as well as master of ceremonies and confirm the date with special guests	
Create a guest list	
Book the photographer/videographer	
Get staff/volunteers to help you if necessary	
2-4 months before	
Book security	
Get insurance	
Launch event website	
List the event on local event websites	
Confirm the menu with caterers/venue	

Book decor, chairs, linens	
Determine whether you need additional permits and apply for them	
Determine any other facilities necessary for the event and book them (eg parking, electrical, lighting, stage, sound system, tents or gazebos, and portable toilets)	
Design the invites and send them out	
Print branded event stationery and gifts, badges or lanyards	
Organise branding for the event (posters, banners, pamphlets)	
Create an official event programme and have it printed	
Less than 2 months before	
Send out reminder invitations	
Send out press releases	

Get social media active if the event needs publicity	
Confirm with any speakers/entertainment	
Put together speaker/guest packs	
1 week before	
Hand our flyers or pamphlets	
Confirm media/press attendance	
Confirm with all vendors	
The day of	
Have a meeting with staff/volunteers to go through the plan of action so everyone knows what they should be doing	
Ensure everything flows smoothly; be on hand to deal with any hiccups	
The day after	

Events are great networking opportunities – use the time afterwards to send thank-you notes to attendees, speakers, special guests and so forth	
Do an event debrief. Take note of what worked and what didn't	

Step 5: Make your event stand out to the crowd

To make an event memorable, it needs to stand out from the rest, so you'll have to get your creative juices flowing. What's more, if this is going to be a career for you, you will have to stand out from other planners. In many cases, event planners may be required to submit proposals for events, in which case you need to be the best.

The possibilities for what you can do differently are endless, so do jot down ideas as they come to you and do lots of research.

Theme

Themes are a great way of adding some personality to any event and engaging the attention of the guests. You can pick a theme that ties into the aim of the event, or try something new and different.

Spruce it up

Little things can be very memorable, so add personal touches and cute ideas for your guests to marvel at, making your event just that little bit more special.

Trends

While you want to keep your event as unique as possible, keep a finger on the pulse of the event planning world to make sure you're up to date on all the latest trends – and then improve on them if you can.

Step 6: Confirm the main attraction

What's the main attraction of your event? Are you going to have speakers or some fun entertainment? Since this will be the "centrepiece" of the event, it's important to get this booked in advance and get written confirmation of the booking. You may also need to put down a deposit.

Speakers/VIPs

If you're inviting a guest speaker, you'll want to make sure to help them with any travel arrangements and accommodation. After confirming the date, make sure to just re-confirm a few weeks before the event, and to keep an eye on all the relevant arrangements.

Entertainment

Choose your entertainment with your guests in mind – things like their age or interests can guide you in the right direction. Also think about the tone of the event – what kind of entertainment will accentuate your goal of how the event should go? Depending on the kind of event you're throwing, this can range from magicians to a ukulele band.

Activities

When you're planning parties, you want to keep the guests engaged and having fun. Interactive activities are a great way to do this – things like photo booths with props at weddings can give guests something to occupy themselves with when the bride and groom are taking photos. See if you can come up with a similarly great idea.

Step 7: Publicity, publicity, publicity

So if the objective of your event is to get people talking, how do you go about generating that kind of publicity? There a few different platforms you can use to your advantage.

Start well in advance by spreading the word, and also provide updates afterwards to increase your reach.

Communication plan

Decide on the channels you are going to use to distribute the message about your event, as well as how frequently and what information should be communicated.

Communication tools

Before you can begin your campaign to make your event known to the world, you have to develop the basics you're going to use. This includes text, images, a logo and a slogan, as well as the formats of your various promotional material. These basic tools should contain everything people need to know about the cause of the event, and you're going to use them everywhere: social media, website, invites, branding, and so forth. Keep the tone of the event in mind when you develop these 'tools'. If your budget allows, you may want to hire a professional.

Communication channels

Social media

Social media is a huge perk we have today in order to create awareness. Decide which platforms will reach the most of your readers and create pages or profiles for them. Update these regularly. Do some research about social media management to make sure you get the most out of the process – things like the times most people are on social media are very useful to keep in mind. You can also keep track of how many people your posts reach, as well as people interested in attending the event, giving you a very comprehensive idea of how well your campaign is doing.

If social media isn't your forte, and getting clued up doesn't sound like a viable plan, you can also hire someone to handle this aspect for you.

Press releases

Gather together a database of media and their email addresses and send out a press release close to the event and afterwards, with some images and information about the event. The press can use this for possible articles. (You will also be sending them invites so they can get a first-hand experience.)

Websites

For an event on a larger scale, with many guests or an open invitation, creating a website is a great way of making information regarding the event available, and confirming attendance. Remember to optimise the website for search engines to give you maximum visibility.

Websites have also become quite popular for weddings.

Flyers and posters

Have a few of these printed out. Stick up posters in high foot traffic areas where people will be able to see them. If you have the budget, billboards are a great idea. Hand out flyers at intersections.

Local event websites

There are a few websites out there that list things going on in the area. Make sure to submit your own event information to these sites.

Ticket sales

If you're selling tickets, either do it on your own website or submit your event to a bigger ticket sales website.

Step 8: Weddings – the work of a love curator

Weddings are a different ball game from other types of events, and can often be quite a bit more eventful and more effort to do successfully because of their unique demands. However, if you are brave enough, here are a few things that set weddings apart from other events:

- **It's someone's special day** For many this is the most important day of their lives, and so tensions can run a little high, and the possibility for handling the unexpected is that much higher.
- **The planning timeframe is longer** Weddings are going to take up more of your time, since the run-up tends to be a lot longer.
- **Weddings all follow the same format** The challenge here is to make it unique and special while still staying within that format.

- **Decorations** Wedding decorations can be quite elaborate, and you will most likely be presented with numerous ideas that you will have to incorporate into the event.

Here's a comprehensive checklist of everything you need to do, and when to do it:

Wedding planning checklist

Couple:	
Date and time:	
Venue:	
Number of guests:	
Briefing	
Have introductory meeting with client to determine their requirements: venue, number of guests, theme and budget as well as any specific requests	
12+ months before	

Confirm final budget	
Confirm estimated number of guests (this will affect which venue is chosen)	
Pick a date and venue (ceremony and reception may be at different places, so there will be two venues)	
Confirm date with officiant and important guests	
Book the venue on the chosen date and pay deposit (get written confirmation)	
Plan and have engagement party	
Have engagement photo shoot	
4-12 months before	
Plan and purchase wedding attire	
Confirm the guest list	
Book the officiant	
Look at accommodation for guests who may need to stay over	

Book the photographer and videographer	
Book the band, musician or DJ	
Book the florist	
Plan menu; hire caterer if necessary	
Open a wedding registry	
Select invitations, save-the-dates and stationery (favours, thank-you cards, menu, seating charts, guest book)	
Send save-the-dates	
Book transportation for wedding party and bride's arrival	
Book facilities: lighting, electrical	
Book decor, chairs, linens	
Schedule cake tastings and order cake	
Purchase wedding rings	
Have pre-wedding photo shoot for wedding stationery and/or other uses at wedding	

Purchase wedding stationery; hire calligrapher if desired	
2-4 months before	
Send out invitations	
Confirm the menu with caterers/venue	
Book accommodation for guests staying over	
Determine any other facilities necessary for the event (eg parking)	
Purchase gifts for guests	
Book make-up artist and stylist	
Purchase items for rice-toss, ring bearer pillow, rose petals for flower girls	
Less than 2 months before	
Prepare and give song list to musician, band or DJ – including which songs must be played for entrance, dance, flower toss, garter toss and so forth	
Organise music for bride's entry at ceremony	

Confirm with all vendors	
Make sure couple has applied for marriage licence	
Put together programme for guests and have it printed	
Review programme with officiant, master of ceremonies and wedding party	
Give final guest count to venue or caterer (include vendors like the photographer; they also have to eat)	
Ensure vendors will be provided with necessary additional facilities (like a stage for the band)	
Plan seating chart	
1 week before	
Follow up with guests who haven't RSVP'd	
Confirm with all vendors	
Plan with photographer: which shots must be taken; what time, any props necessary	
Rehearse ceremony proceedings with relevant parties	

The day of	
Arrive at venue early, and supervise setup of ceremony and reception. Ensure everything flows smoothly; be on hand to deal with any hiccups	
The day after	
Clean up venue and return any equipment/decoration hired	

Step 9: The little things are the biggest part

Once you've gotten the bigger things out of the way, like securing a venue and entertainment, it's time to work on the details. Just like the main look of the event will create a big impact, the little things will all add up to make the event that much better.

Photographer

A good photographer will document the event perfectly. This gives you images you can use afterwards for any remaining publicity. Especially if organising a wedding, the photographer is of paramount importance, since the photos are the only thing besides memories that will remain of the day.

Photographers are quite numerous, so you'll have a host of options to choose from. Always check a photographer's portfolio to make sure they are exactly what you're looking for. You may want to do this well in advance as well, as for weddings the couple may want to do an engagement shoot and party, or have a photo session before the wedding to use the images on the invites or at the ceremony. This way your photos will all follow the same look and style.

Invites

There are many different ways to do invitations, and many ways to send them. Consider who the guests are – do you have their addresses, their email addresses? Keep this in mind for the format in which you want to present the invites.

By the time you get to your invites, you would already have chosen some kind of theme for the event, or would know what the pervasive feeling of the event should be. Brief the designer of your invites on this. If your budget doesn't allow for having the invites professionally designed, consider getting a template off the internet, or buying ready-made ones and filling in the details yourself. If you're very creative, you could attempt doing them yourself.

For a corporate event, the best way to send invitations is via email.

Things to include in an invite:

- Name of guest and partner (or just plus one)
- Time and date
- Dress code
- Address and directions
- RSVP date and contact details

- Details about the event (who is speaking/what is the fundraiser for, and so forth). For many corporate events, the invite includes a press release.

Stationery

For some events you'll want to have some stationery on the tables for invitees to use for notes. This is a great opportunity for branding, so make sure to get the logo of the company throwing the event onto things like pens, pencils and notepads, which they can also take home.

Speaker/guest packs

Put together packs to hand out to those attending, as well as special packs for speakers. They can take these home, giving your event more impact after it is done. These should include the following:

- Business cards
- Pamphlets
- Programmes/agendas (see below)
- Branded lanyard or badge (see below)

Lanyards/badges

Some events will need to identify guests by their names and give them some kind of pass. Lanyards and badges are a great way to do this. They can be handed out when guests sign in at the door.

Programmes/agendas

When guests won't know what they can expect at the event, print out some agendas and distribute them at the event (remembering to keep it in line with your theme). Alternatively, they can be emailed with the invitation or sent out close to the event. A run-through should also be provided by the host or master of ceremonies.

Host/master of ceremonies

Most events will need some kind of host to keep attendees aware of what's going on, and to introduce people before they come on stage. While many times this will be some sort of senior person from the company throwing the event, sometimes you will also need to hire someone take care of this.

Audiovisual

Make sure you have all the audio and visual aids necessary for the event ready on the day. These can include projectors, music or microphones and speakers.

Food

There's nothing people love quite as much as free food, but beware if that food doesn't taste great. Remember to cater for all dietary requirements, including vegetarians and vegans, halaal, lactose and gluten intolerance, and paleo. For shorter events, some canapés will do the trick. For longer, more formal events, a set three-course menu might be more appropriate. Remember to taste the event's menu beforehand so you know exactly what kind of quality you'll be getting.

Alternatively, you may want to get vendors to sell food at the event. Find out what facilities the vendors require when you book them and make sure to cater for everything. Ensure a variety of food choices. Check that the vendors have the necessary health and safety certificate (certificate of acceptability) or liquor licence if required.

Registrations

If you need people attending the event to register their details, point them towards the website and have them do it online. Be sure to include any free stuff they'll receive at the event, like branded t-shirts and a three-course dinner. If this is an annual event, you have the perk of sending out new prompts for registration to the previous years' participants.

Alternatively, have a register present at the door when they enter the venue to sign in when they receive their welcome packs.

Permits

If you're using a non-conventional space for your event, or arranging something on a large scale, you may need certain permits (food, noise, road closures), which will be specific to where the event is held.

Additional equipment

Make a list of any additional equipment needed for the event, and check whether your chosen venue has everything needed. Otherwise, book the additional equipment from vendors. These can include a stage, sound system, tents or gazebos, lighting, and portable toilets. Remember to keep all confirmations in writing.

Safety

Large events may need some sort of first aid presence.

Insurance

It's always possible for disaster to strike, so you can speak to your insurance company about insuring the event. People also do this for weddings.

Security

While these might be limited to car guards, if there will be large crowds and large amounts of cash, some type of security may be necessary.

Cleaning staff

For before and after the event, as well as during at the public bathrooms.

Staff

Setting up before and packing up after events can be a huge chore, and you may need extra hands. If you can't find volunteers, hire someone. Think about whether you will need help during the event as well. Brief the staff or volunteers very well before the event, and have a way of keeping in contact (two-way radios, handing out contact lists with all relevant phone numbers).

Step 10: On the big day

When the big day arrives, and it's your first run at event planning, the morning of might see you feeling the flutter of gentle butterfly wings inside your stomach, or possibly the feeling that you swallowed a tumble dryer. But take a deep breath and relax! If you've planned properly, you've already done the hardest part. Unfortunately, this will be where the unexpected might happen – your keynote speaker misses his flight, it starts pouring down on your garden party, or the bride has one too many glasses of champagne.

This is where crisis management comes into play. As part of your thorough planning, you should have contingency plans in case of disaster, because it can, and often does, happen. If the event goes down a path you hadn't anticipated, you have to know what to do. (Unless you're particularly good at thinking on your feet.)

Step 11: Post-event duties

The event may be done, but you're job isn't. For corporate events, you have to send out thank-yous to your guests and any special parties who attended the event or assisted you in any way, and if you were attempting to get some kind of commitment from the guests for a work-related event, you will have to follow up with them.

If you've created a theme or style for the event, stick to that when you compile your thank-you notes. The easiest way to deliver them is via email. Of course, if you have the budget, and you really want to make an impression, you can send a hand-written note on special stationery, and possibly include a small gift.

Update your social media or website afterwards, or send out another press release. This time you'll have lots of photos to include.

Step 12: Debrief

This is a very important step, especially if you're going to do more events in the future. The point of a debrief is to see what worked well, and if the event can be considered a success.

Go back to the questionnaire you did in Step 1 and see whether you accomplished the objectives you set for yourself. Did your event meet all those criteria? If it fell short in any way, determine how you could have changed that aspect to be more successful.

With some events, success is quite easy to judge. With parties and weddings, the measure of their success is simply how much the guests enjoyed it; was it a lively event with everyone partaking and leaving late, or were there to many aspects of it that were subpar, with little participation and guests leaving relatively early? With fundraisers and publicity events, it's not always that simple to establish whether the event was a success. In order to do so, you'll have to put in a little more effort. If the event was heavily marketed on social media, use these same platforms to monitor feedback. If you were trying to raise money, determine how much profit was made and whether it was worth it. When you get in touch with guests to thank them for attendance and to follow up with them, find out whether they enjoyed it. You can even send a survey to the guests.

Chapter 3
Build on what you know

Once you have planned your first event and done a debrief on it, you will have begun to learn what works, and what doesn't. Start compiling this information into a database that you can work from in the future, to make every event more successful than the last. Build up your contacts, and keep the information of venues, photographers and entertainers that truly stood out from the rest. Build relationships with them.

Keep a comprehensive book or computer file (preferably both so you have a back-up), listing all your important contacts and information. Organise it by chapter for ease of use, and keep some photos of the events and decorations, so that you can refer back to certain ideas. Also include a list of all the events you do according to type, and provide rundowns and debriefs of how the events went, so that you can keep track of what was most successful.

Remember, it's all about organised planning!

Conclusion

Whether you're embarking on a career of planning, or just upgrading your skill set to include being a master of fabulous events, I hope this book can be your trusty little go-to guide – a little compass to keep you going in the right direction when you're feeling a bit overwhelmed or lost.

Good luck!

Thank you again for downloading this book!

If you would like another book in a similar category, please visit my author page at amazon.com/author/joshuanathan

Finally, if you enjoyed this book, please take the time to share your thoughts and post a review on Amazon, It'd be greatly appreciated!

Now go live your life to the fullest – and relish every moment of it!

Thank you and good luck!

http://www.mellowzoo.com

Read on for previews to other books we think will benefit you!

Preview of: "Time Management: 12 Simple Time Management Steps to Better Focus, Faster Progress and Optimal Results"

"Productivity is not just about doing more, it is about creating more impact with less work."

– Prima Malik

Time is a finite commodity; we have only the allotted number of hours in a day
to get things done. And if you're anything like the millions of people out there
trying to keep up in this always-on, always-connected digital age, it might
seem like those hours just aren't enough.

But what if you changed the way you used those hours? The simple fact is
that successful people manage their time better. It's not about trying to do
more, it's about streamlining what you're already doing – focusing enough
time on the right tasks – and in that way opening up more time for other
pursuits, like those things you've always wanted to do, but can never get
around to.

That's the topic this book explores: harnessing good time management,
sharper focus and correct planning to make every 24 hours as productive as
they can possibly be. It's really that easy. You just need to change your
approach.

So if you're ready to super-charge what you're really capable of accomplishing every day, let's get started!

Download on my author page on amazon
amazon.com/author/joshuanathan

PREVIEW OF: "MINDFULNESS: BE PRESENT, SAVOUR EVERY MOMENT AND LIVE A HAPPIER LIFE IN 12 SIMPLE STEPS"

"Most humans are never fully present in the now, because unconsciously they believe that the next moment must be more important than this one. But then you miss your whole life, which is never not now. And that's a revelation for some people: to realise that your life is only ever now."

– Eckhart Tolle

Think about how much time you spend walking around on auto-pilot, only ever paying attention when someone says your name. What's happening around you right now – the sounds, the smells, the atmosphere. Have you noticed any of it?

It's time to become **mindful** – noticing, experiencing and appreciating the present more; learning to savour the moment and create more memorable ones; reinforcing bonds with the people in your life by paying attention to them; taking care of your body and mind the way they deserve; and easing the stress of everyday living by increasing your understanding of yourself.

This book is an aid to help you snap out of it for good, and actually live in the moment. After all, the only time that really exists is the present. It's all you have, and all you ever will have. You cannot change the past; and the future is forever out of reach. Life is such a precious gift – stop letting it pass you by.

Try these 12 simple steps, and I guarantee you'll walk out of the experience with a new perspective – and hopefully as a happier, less stressed and more present human being, who'll live a fuller life as a consequence.

So are you ready to live in the moment? Let's get started!

Download on my author page on amazon
amazon.com/author/joshuanathan

PREVIEW OF: "SLEEP SECRETS: 12 SIMPLE TIME MANAGEMENT STEPS TO BETTER FOCUS, FASTER PROGRESS AND OPTIMAL RESULTS"

And so it begins

It's 2 o'clock on a Monday morning. You're still awake. Wide awake. Staring at the ceiling yet again, worrying every 10 minutes about how much time you have left to sleep before you have to get up for work. The more you try to close your eyes and concentrate on falling asleep, the harder it seems to be. It's a vicious circle. You're exhausted and frustrated, but your brain just won't 'click' off.

I've been there, for 6 months I relied on the little sleep I got to keep functioning. If I managed 4 hours it was a great night, but when it started dropping to 2 hours, then 1 hour, then 20 minutes, I knew I had to do something! Anything! I was in a state of turmoil, and it seemed as though nothing was helping which simply made my frustration worse. It started affecting my mood, my work and my relationships. I had to find a way. I took months trying to figure out what it was that was keeping me awake, I was willing to try anything out of sheer desperation.

Then one day I got it right.

If like me, you are at that point where you are feeling frustrated and you just need to sleep, then this book is for you. I have taken the time to meticulously compile everything I've tried into one small, easy to follow guide in the hopes that my experiences could somehow help you. You will learn how to give yourself every advantage to fall asleep, from getting your environment ready to monitoring your patterns with a sleep log and trying various techniques on how to relax a busy mind.

The purpose of this book is purely to help you figure out what is keeping you
awake and how we can possibly fix that together.

So if you're ready for some serious shuteye then let's get started!

Download on my author page on amazon
amazon.com/author/joshuanathan

www.ingramcontent.com/pod-product-compliance
Lightning Source LLC
Chambersburg PA
CBHW070338190526
45169CB00005B/1945